Farm-to-Table Success
A Guide for Launching a Sustainable-Agri Business

Table of Contents

Chapter 1. Introduction

Dive into the vibrant and fulfilling world of sustainable farming with our Special Report on "Farm-to-Table Success: A Guide for Launching a Sustainable-Agri Business." This in-depth exploration is a must-have for those interested in sowing seeds both in the soil and the community, innovatively bridging the gap between farm and fork. Whether you're an experienced rancher, a budding farmer, or even a city dweller with an interest in sustainable business, this comprehensive guide will educate, inspire, and equip you to partake in this blossoming economic sector. Presented in a manner that brings the joy of farming to life, our report is not just about information; it's about the promise of nurturing nature, growing businesses and creating a healthier, more connected world. Don't miss this chance to plant roots of change; get your guide to launching a successful sustainable-agri business today!

Chapter 2. Understanding the Farm-to-Table Movement

The farm-to-table movement is more than just a hip trend; it's a fundamental shift towards sustainable, community-focused agriculture that seeks to diminish traditional supply chains and provide consumers with fresh, local, and nutritionally superior food options. It necessitates a unique approach to food production, distribution, and consumption, and is based on fostering relationships between consumers and the community of farmers, ranchers, and fishermen who are responsively and sustainably producing our food.

2.1. The Ethical Root of the Movement

Farm-to-table, in its purest form, is a food system wherein food is locally sourced, with few intermediaries between the farmer and the consumer, traditionally embodied through restaurants working directly with local farms. This reconnection to the sources of our food was borne out of concern for industrial-scale farming's impact on health, economies, and the environment.

Where conventional food systems unwittingly disconnected consumers from the people who grew their food, farm-to-table attempts to repair that rupture. This system values the relationship between farmers, cooks, and consumers and converts it into a food story that evokes feelings of community, trust, sustainability, and respect for the food and the environment.

2.2. The Journey from Industrial to Sustainable Agriculture

Post World War II saw the rise of large-scale, industrialized farming, promising improved convenience and efficiency. It was viewed as a remedy to world hunger, capable of providing abundant food at lower costs. However, this model soon revealed its flaws. Industrial farming practices led to a decrease in food diversity, reliance on chemical fertilizers and pesticides, and degradation of the soil and the environment.

The farm-to-table movement originated in the 1970s as a counteraction to these practices, bringing attention back towards sustainable farming methods that respect the Earth and the integrity of our food. Pioneer food activists, like Alice Waters of the famed Chez Panisse restaurant in Berkeley, California, passionately advocated for organic, fresh, and locally obtained ingredients. Her efforts were grounded in the idea that food is a collective experience and should therefore be derived from local communities to provide maximum freshness and nutrition, and reduce carbon footprint.

2.3. Nuances of the Farm-to-Table Model

Farm-to-table encourages a multifaceted relationship between the community and local farmers, the nuances of which can be gleaned from:

1. *Proximity* – The closer the source of food, the fresher and more nutritious it is. Preserving the climate, soil type, and region-specific conditions in which the food is grown and consumed can also contribute positively to one's health.

2. *Seasonality* – Following the ebb and flow of natural growing

seasons ensures that food is full of flavor and nutrients. It explicitly challenges the norm of having every type of produce available all year round, showing respect for the environment's natural rhythm.

3. *Sustainability* – The movement encourages farming practices that protect biodiversity, foster healthy ecosystems, reduce water usage, and minimize the carbon footprint.

4. *Transparency* – Farm-to-table promotes an open dialogue between producers and consumers, ultimately heightening awareness and understanding about where our food comes from.

5. *Community Empowerment* – The movement strengthens local economies, creating jobs and fostering respect for hard-working farmers, whose noble occupation has often been overlooked in the Industrial age.

2.4. The Economic Impact and Challenges of the Model

Farm-to-table has the potential to transform not only the way we eat but also local economies. It redirects the profits from multi-national corporations to local farmers, thereby leading to community development and encouraging the growth of smaller farms.

However, it's not without its challenges. Logistical complexities and costs associated with coordinating directly with multiple small farms are considerable. Although potentially workable for individual restaurants, it is much harder to implement at scale. Enterprises need to be ready to invest time, effort, and money into this endeavor to make it truly sustainable and beneficial to all involved.

2.5. Farm-to-Table: A Guide to Getting Involved

You don't need to be a farmer or a professional chef to be involved in the farm-to-table movement. As a consumer, you can proactively support local farmers by buying produce at your local farmers' markets and eating at farm-to-table restaurants. You could also consider joining a CSA (Community Supported Agriculture) scheme, which lets you subscribe to a seasonal selection of fresh, local produce directly from your local farmer.

By understanding the farm-to-table movement, we carve out a path to a better, healthier world, that not only employs sustainable farming methods but also supports local economies. It bridges the gap between the farmer and the consumer, creating a community centered around fresh, valuable food. It won't happen overnight, but with each local apple bought, each seasonal menu savored, and each farming story shared, we reaffirm the importance of this extraordinary movement - signifying a commitment to wholesome, nourishing food, respect for our environment, and love for our community.

Chapter 3. Why Sustainable-Agriculture Matters

In recent years there is an unfolding transition from traditional agronomic practices to more sustainable methods, fueled by mounting concerns regarding climate change, depleting resources, and an overarching need to ensure food security for a growing population. A switch to sustainable farming offers a practical solution, blending essential farming practices with innovative technology and ecological sensibility.

3.1. Understanding the Core of Sustainable Agriculture

Sustainable agriculture is a multifaceted approach targeting the long-term sustainability of the natural environment, the agricultural economy, and the food supply. At its core is a dedication to three fundamental pillars: eco-friendly practices, economic profitability, and social & economic equity. These pillars can be likened to a three-legged stool, where each contributes to the overall stability of the sustainable agriculture system.

Eco-friendly practices incorporate every operational step that promotes a cycle of beneficial biodiversity. These include maintaining healthy soil, managing water wisely, minimizing air, water, and climate pollution, and promoting diversity of plants and animals.

Economic profitability implies that farmers engaged in sustainable practices can be financially competitive with traditional farmers. Not only do these practices reduce expenses and increase profits through efficient use of resources and reduced chemical input, but they also open up new markets focused on locally grown and organic foods.

Social and economic equity denotes fair treatment of all those involved in the agricultural process — farmers, ranchers, workers, their families, and communities. It recognises their right to quality life and a safe, healthy working environment.

3.2. The Environmental Impact of Sustainable Agriculture

The environmental advantages of adopting sustainable agricultural practices are numerous. Here are some key highlights:

1. Reduce Soil Erosion: Healthy soil is the backbone of any farming enterprise, but traditional farming practices often lead to severe soil erosion. Sustainable farming methods such as crop rotation, cover cropping, and organic fertilizers help maintain soil health, enrich soil fertility, and prevent soil erosion.

2. Conserving Water: Sustainable farming also champions water conservation through efficient irrigation systems such as drip irrigation, soaker hoses, or the use of rain barrels. Such efficient use of water reduces wastage and ensures plants get the right amount of water when they need it.

3. Enhancing Biodiversity: Sustainable farming contributes to biodiversity by fostering a variety of plants and animals. By employing practices like growing multiple crops, farmers create a more balanced and diverse ecosystem that can support a wide variety of wildlife, contributing to a healthier environment.

4. Mitigating Climate Change: As sustainable farming avoids synthetic fertilizers and pesticides, the associated greenhouse gas emissions are lowered.

3.3. The Economic Potential of Sustainable Agriculture

Sustainable farming can also offer substantial economic potential. As consumers become more environmentally conscious, the market for sustainably-produced food grows. A commitment to sustainable farming allows for a wider variety of crops, increased drought resistance, and ultimately, a reliable yield. Even in the face of climate variation, sustainable farming practices ensure productivity and keep the agricultural economy flourishing.

The economic gains also extend to farmers who are spared the escalating costs of chemical inputs and potentially damaging lawsuits that can result from chemical exposure or contamination.

3.4. Social Equity and Sustainable Agriculture

Sustainable agriculture is also an ally for social equity. Farmers are able to command higher prices for organically grown produce, benefiting from a model that respects human health and conservation. Farm workers avoid exposure to harmful pesticides and unhealthy farming practices. Also, communities find safer, healthier food options in their local markets.

It's not just about physical health; sustainable farming bolsters social well-being too. It fosters community ties as the farmer-consumer relationship is reaffirmed in farmer's markets or cooperatives. More people reconnect with their land and heritage, and rural communities become revitalized.

In sum, sustainable agriculture isn't just a concept or a trend. It's a system of practices and methods that bring a wide array of benefits to our environment, our economy, and our society as a whole. The bottom line is, sustainable agriculture matters because our future depends on it. As individuals, we have a role to play. We can choose to support sustainable farming practices, buy organic foods, and champion for policies that will shift our agricultural industry towards this more sustainable course. These are essential steps towards a healthier, more sustainable future.

Chapter 4. Assessing Your Resources: Land, Labor and Capital

Understanding what resources you have and how to utilize them is integral when starting a sustainable-agri business. It's essential to assess the three key components: land, labor, and capital. These are the pillars upon which your business will stand, and understanding them will ensure the success and sustainability of your venture.

4.1. Land - The Foundation

The first and foremost resource you need to consider is your land. It's not just about the quantity but also the quality and type of land you have. Understandably, recognition of soil quality, climate conditions, water source, and local biodiversity should be the initial steps of your strategic plan.

The soil is your most important natural resource. Essential factors such as its texture, structure, and fertility can drastically affect your farming activities. Conduct a detailed soil test by either sending soil samples to a certified laboratory or using do-it-yourself kits. The test will reveal the soil's pH level, nutrient content, water-holding capacity, and potentially harmful elements, guiding you in selecting suitable crops.

Climate conditions and their fluctuations impact the choice of crops and farming practices. Information about local weather, including temperature patterns, seasonal rainfall, and intensity of sunlight, should be gathered and studied thoroughly.

Water availability is vital. Evaluate your water resources, understand their quality and seasonal availability. If your land doesn't have natural water sources, explore options like rainwater harvesting, dug wells, and borewells.

Consider the local biodiversity as well. The presence of beneficial animals and insects can contribute to the health and vitality of your farm. Equally, understanding local pests can help to develop effective control systems.

4.2. Labor - The Work Force

Labor is another critical component in farming. Deciding between using family labor, hiring local workers, or both, will also be a deciding factor in your farming practices. This decision is influenced by factors such as the farm's size, the type of crops, and the farming methods you implement.

Family labor is usually more reliable and less expensive. However, the skills and physical abilities of family members may limit the range of tasks they can perform. Balancing between labor-intensive tasks and tasks that require specialized skills can dictate the level of outside help needed.

Recruiting the local workforce can promote social and economic stability within your community. However, take into consideration that hiring workers implicates legal responsibilities and financial implications such as wages, taxes, and insurance.

To efficiently manage labor, establish a robust plan that includes schedules for critical tasks, worker safety measures, and effective communication methods.

4.3. Capital - Fuel for Growth

Capital is the financial resource needed to start and run your farm. This includes cash reserves, credit facilities, and any other sources of funding available to you.

Firstly, assess your personal savings. These can be used for purchasing land, equipment, seeds, and also for operating expenses such as labor and utilities. This is the safest type of capital as it does not require repayment.

Next, consider potential borrowing options. This includes loans from banks or credit unions, lines of credit, and credit cards. Remember, borrowed money must be paid back with interest and usually requires some form of collateral as safety.

Furthermore, explore governmental schemes and grants. Many governments offer subsidies and grants to support sustainable-agri farming as it promotes environmental conservation and helps ensure food security. Be aware that these often come with conditions that must be met.

Lastly, potential investors and partnerships could provide capital. Investors can offer large sums of money, business expertise, and valuable connections in return for a stake in your business. Partnerships can pool resources and share risks but require careful legal considerations.

Defining your capital resources will help formulate your business plan by providing a clear picture of the financial resources available, planned expenditures, and projected income.

By conducting a careful evaluation of these three key resources – land, labor, and capital – you will establish a strong foundation for your sustainable-agri business. The knowledge and insights gained from this process will help you lay the groundwork, set realistic goals, and create a strategic plan for operating a successful and sustainable farm.

Chapter 5. Mapping Your Agri-business Model

Diving into the details of your prospective agri-business requires an understanding that this is not just a business - it's a lifestyle commitment that impacts not only your livelihood, but also your community and the environment. Therefore, conducting proper groundwork is fundamental.

5.1. Understanding Your Core Mission

Before you begin, it's essential to clarify what drives your desire to venture into sustainable farming. Your core mission should resonate both at a personal level and an organizational one. It might be rooted in wanting to contribute to food security, promote a healthier diet, biodiversity preservation, reducing environmental degradation, or working within the realms of a circular economy.

Understand what you're passionate about, as this passion will fuel your work even when challenges arise. List down these core purposes and keep them at the forefront of your planning process.

5.2. Identifying the Core Product or Service

Next, identify the core product or service you plan to offer. Do you want to focus on organic vegetable farming? Are you more inclined towards poultry? Perhaps your interest leans towards fodder crops? Or maybe you're captivated by the idea of starting an apiary? Whatever your focus, write it down and study it well. Read as much as you can; talk to experts in that area; visit farms that specialize in your area of interest if possible.

5.3. Business Model Sketch

Once the core product or service has been defined, you need to start sketching your business model. This includes identifying your key partners, key activities, key resources, customer segments, channels, customer relationships, cost structure, and revenue streams.

It's advisable to document this into the Business Model Canvas. While the Business Model Canvas is typically created for conventional businesses, it works remarkably well for an agri-business too. Its structure prompts you to ask the right questions at the right time.

5.4. Market Analysis

Identifying your potential customers and understanding their needs is fundamental. Explore the consumer behavior in your target market, identify consumer trends, and determine their willingness to pay for sustainable, locally sourced products.

Consider conducting surveys to understand your customers better, or maybe join local community meetings and events to foster relationships and gain insights into what the community members may need and want from a business like yours.

5.5. Setting Sustainable Goals and Objectives

To ensure that your agri-business is sustainable in every way, set goals that prioritize sustainability along with profitability. These goals will serve as your roadmap - illuminating the path to a resilient business model that values and enhances both your bank balance and the environment.

Set objectives that are specific, measurable, achievable, relevant, and time-bound (SMART). They might pertain to minimizing the use of non-renewable resources, enhancing biodiversity on your farm, minimizing waste, or empowering your local community.

5.6. Legal and Monetary Considerations

Remember that your agri-business, like any business, will need to adhere to federal, state, and local regulations for agriculture and business operations. You'll need to understand these regulations and include them in your planning.

Let's also not forget that, just as a tree needs sun and water to grow, an agri-business requires funds to thrive. Proper financial planning is thus pertinent. Create a financial model of your business, including projections of costs, revenues, cash flows, and profitability.

5.7. The Farming Operation Plan

This includes the details of the day-to-day farming operations. You need to strategize your crop rotation system, pest management plan, harvest schedule, and other farming activities. Implementing sustainable farming practices and technologies at this stage promotes a circular economy that values waste and regenerates natural systems.

5.8. From Farm to Table

Lastly, the goal is to create a bridge between your farm and the customers' table. Accordingly, create a robust supply chain management plan. This can include collaborating with local businesses, farmers markets, or setting up an online presence. Strategizing this final step of 'Farm to Table' is crucial to creating a successful agri-business.

In conclusion, mapping your agri-business model is not a small task. It requires a lot of research, contemplation, and planning. But with clear objectives and a commitment to your mission, you can undoubtedly create a sustainable, profitable, and fulfilling business. You will sow the seeds of change, nurture your community, and reap the fruitful rewards of sustainable farming.

After all, as author Richard Louv said, "Doing right by the earth-and right by ourselves-are one and the same mission." Let your agri-business be a beacon of that mission.

Chapter 6. Sowing the Seeds: Choosing the Right Crops

Choosing the right crop is arguably the most critical decision when initiating your journey into sustainable farming. Many factors influence this decision, including the local climate, soil suitability, market demand, and most importantly, your personal interests and goals. This comprehensive exploration will unpack the considerations you need to make to ensure that you are sowing the seeds that will ultimately reap profits, sustainability, and joy.

6.1. Understanding Your Soil

Before you can select the right crops, you must first understand your soil. Soil quality significantly impacts crop performance and yield.

To begin this process, take soil samples from your future planting site at different depths. These samples should be tested for nutrient content, pH balance, and organic matter percentage. However, keep in mind that results may slightly vary due to nutrients being mobile in the environment. Send your samples to a certified laboratory to get the most accurate results.

Also, it's crucial to understand the soil structure or texture. Soil texture categorizes soil based on proportions of sand, silt, and clay. Different plants have different soil texture preferences. For instance, root vegetables like loamy soil, while leafy vegetables tend to prefer soil with higher clay content.

6.2. Local Climate and Seasonality

In addition to understanding your soil, knowledge of your local climate is crucial. Temperature ranges, length of growing seasons, and precipitation levels will all play a significant role in determining which crops are appropriate for your area.

Research local climate data to understand which plant hardiness zone you fall into. This data can guide you in choosing the plants most likely to thrive in your specific conditions. Understanding frost dates will also inform your planting and harvesting schedules.

6.3. Market Demand and Profitability

Next, understanding your local market demand for various crops can help guide your decision. Your ability to sell the crops you grow is central to the success of your farming business.

Begin by researching your local market: What sells well? What is under-supplied? Engaging with local restaurants, grocers, and farmers market coordinators can provide insights into current crop trends and demands. Also, consider the potential for direct sales to consumers through Community Supported Agriculture (CSA) programs or farm stands.

Along with demand, profitability is a crucial consideration. Various crops have different input costs (seeds, fertilizes, pest control), labor requirements, and potential sales prices.

6.4. Personal Preferences and Interests

Though it might seem trivial in comparison to factors like soil and climate, your personal interest and passion for certain crops are essential to sustained motivation and satisfaction.

Farming demands considerable physical effort and mental resolve.

Cultivating crops you love makes these demands worthwhile and can ultimately contribute to your business's longevity.

6.5. Experimentation

After considering all the factors mentioned above, it may feel overwhelming to settle with a few crops. One approach is to start with a small, diverse selection of crops that meet your criteria for soil, climate, market demand, and personal interest. After you have some experience with this variety, you can make adjustments based on your observations.

6.6. The Role of Crop Rotation

Crop rotation improves soil fertility and helps manage pests and diseases. It involves changing the type of crop grown in a specific field each year or season.

Planning your crop rotation pattern before planting saves time and further promotes sustainable farming practices. The most basic crop rotation plan involves alternating families of vegetables each year. For instance, you could plant a bed with legumes one year and rotate to a brassica like cabbage or kale the next.

In conclusion, choosing the right crops is a multifaceted decision that involves understanding your soil, considering local climate and market demand, assessing your personal interests, and the willingness to experiment and adapt over time. It sets the foundation for a successful farm-to-table sustainable agri-business. Embrace this process with patience, enjoyment, and a readiness to learn, and you'll nurture a farm that not only grows crops but also your connection to the land and the community around you.

Chapter 7. Innovative Farming Techniques for Sustainability

The growth and popularity of sustainable farming have been fueled by the increasing need for food systems that minimize harm to the environment and human health. At the heart of sustainable agriculture lies a wide range of innovative farming techniques aimed at promoting environmental health, economic profitability, and social and economic equity. These methods strive not only to reduce the impact of farming on the environment but also improve productivity and the quality of the produce.

7.1. Integrating Crop and Livestock Systems

Integrated crop and livestock systems involve the use of the two sectors in a mutually beneficial relationship. These systems utilize crop residues and byproducts as feed for animals and animal manure as a source of nutrients for crop production. This reduces the need for synthetic fertilizers and feeds, which are not only expensive but also present environmental and health risks when used excessively.

One promising practice in integrated crop-livestock systems is the rotation of crops and livestock on the same land. This diversified system allows for a balanced nutrient cycle, pest suppression, and risk distribution, leading to increased productivity and efficiency.

7.2. Conservation Agriculture

Conservation agriculture is a farming technique centered on improving soil health. It includes three main principles: minimal soil disturbance, permanent soil cover, and diversified crop rotations. By reducing tillage, the soil structure is maintained, enabling better water and nutrient retention. Permanent soil cover, usually through the use of cover crops, reduces soil erosion, enhances soil organic matter, and provides habitats for beneficial organisms. Diversified crop rotations break the cycle of pests and diseases, as different crops attract different species.

7.3. Polyculture and Agroforestry

Polyculture, the opposite of monoculture, involves growing multiple crops in the same space, mimicking the diversity found in natural ecosystems. This approach increases biodiversity, enhances resilience to pests, and improves nutrient cycling.

Agroforestry, on the other hand, is a land use management system where trees or shrubs are grown around or among crops or pastureland. These trees can provide shelter and food for a variety of wildlife, increase carbon sequestration, and provide secondary crops that can diversify farm income.

7.4. Organic Farming

Rather than relying on synthetic chemical inputs, organic farming relies on natural processes and inputs for crop production. This includes the use of compost, cover crops, and biopesticides as alternatives to synthetic fertilizers, herbicides, and pesticides. A crucial component of organic farming is the conservation and enhancement of soil health, creating a virtuous cycle of improved fertility and crop growth.

7.5. Permaculture

Permaculture is another innovative farming technique focused on the development of agricultural ecosystems that are sustainable and self-sufficient. Permaculture design principles include observation of nature, recognition of patterns and relationships, and using biological resources, all leading to food production systems that require minimal external inputs.

7.6. Aquaponics and Hydroponics

Aquaponics is an innovative system that combines aquaculture (raising aquatic animals such as fish) with hydroponics (cultivating plants in water without soil). The waste from the fish provides organic nutrients for plants, and the plants naturally filter the water for the fish, creating a sustainable cycle.

Hydroponics, in contrast, is a soil-less farming technique where plants are grown in nutrient-rich water solution. These systems can be incredibly space and resource-efficient, making them a suitable choice for urban farming.

7.7. The Internet of Things (IoT) in Farming

Modern farming is increasingly embracing technology. IoT can help in automating farming processes, tracking and analyzing data like temperature, rainfall, humidity, wind speed, soil pH, and nutrient levels. It provides a precision farming approach where decisions are data-driven, reducing waste of resources and improving yield quality and quantity.

Sustainable farming isn't a singular technique but rather a collection of innovative methods and ideologies that work in harmony with nature. It's a commitment to responsible farming, not just for the betterment of yields and income, but for the welfare of generations to come. By thoroughly understanding and implementing these techniques, one can set the foundation for a successful farm-to-table business.

Chapter 8. Harvesting and Processing Your Produce

Farming operations are a dancing cycle of planning, sowing, nurturing, and finally, the crescendo of harvesting. However, the intricacies of harvesting and processing your produce are much more than simply taking the fruit of your labor to the market. This section explores the diverse aspects of this phase, including detailed best practices for harvesting, considerations about processing, and insight into efficient storage methodologies.

8.1. Best Practices for Harvesting

Healthy crops are directly related to successful harvesting practices. Timing your harvests, employing appropriate methods, and maintaining strict hygiene standards are all essential components.

The first consideration in harvesting your crops is the timing. Though each crop might have specific considerations, generally, vegetables are at their peak nutritional value just prior to maturity. Fruits too, but with some variation depending on the variety, should best be picked when they are fully colored but not entirely ripe. This provides them some time to reach full maturity during the post-harvest period.

Tools are a critical part of harvesting. Use sharp, clean harvesting scissors or hand pruners for delicate crops, like leafy greens or tomatoes. For root crops, such as carrots or potatoes, a sturdy spade or fork works well. The cleanliness of the tools you use is as important as the tool choice. Regularly wash and disinfect your harvesting tools to avoid cross-contamination and the spread of diseases.

Then comes the crucial aspect of handling. Handle your fruits and vegetables gently to prevent bruising, as it can lead to rapid spoilage. It's advisable to sort your produce into grades or types immediately after harvesting, which aids in the further processing and marketing processes. While sorting, bear in mind factors like size, color, maturity, and overall quality.

8.2. Processing Your Harvest

After harvesting, most fruits and vegetables generally require some type of processing. This stage transforms your raw produce into the final product ready for consumption or sale. Depending on the type of produce and your end market, these processing steps could include washing, drying, trimming, peeling, slicing, and packaging.

Washing your produce thoroughly straight after harvesting helps remove any dirt, chemicals, or small pests. As much as possible, use cold running water for the washing process. Soaking should be avoided, as it could lead to increased water absorption by the produce, negatively affecting its shelf life.

In some cases, particularly with herbs and leafy greens, drying is an important step post-washing. A salad spinner comes in handy to remove the excess water without damaging the leaves.

Trimming and peeling are selective procedures, often necessary for crops like carrots, beetroots, or potatoes. Remember, the less you peel off, the more the nutrients are retained in your food.

Your processed items might be consumed directly, or you may choose to add value by transforming raw items into products like jams, pickles, dried fruits, or sauces. While such techniques could command higher market prices, they also involve potential considerations about food safety standards and licensing requirements.

Lastly, how you package your produce significantly impacts its market value and shelf life. Using sustainable packaging materials can add further appeal to your products from a sustainability standpoint.

8.3. Storing Harvested Produce

Efficient storage plays a crucial role in mitigating post-harvest losses. The key points of storing produce are maintaining appropriate temperature, humidity, and proper ventilation. Typically, cold and humid conditions are best for most fruits and vegetables.

Refrigeration may be required for certain produce like leafy greens, strawberries, or fresh beans. This can help in slowing down the oxidation process and preventing the produce from wilting or becoming inedible.

For long-term storage, techniques such as canning, freezing, and drying can be employed. Remember that every fruit or vegetable has individual storage needs, so research and planning go hand in hand with successful storage.

In conclusion, harvesting, processing, and storage of your farm's yield are an art that combines science, timing, and gut instinct, honed over time. Mastering these steps can significantly enhance the success of your sustainable farming business. As you reap the rewards of your farm-to-table venture, you are making a difference not just to your own life but also contributing to a healthier community and a sustainable world.

Chapter 9. Building Relationships: Connecting with Local Markets and Restaurants

Sustainable farming is an endeavor rooted in connection - it's about fostering healthy relationships between yourself, your farm, your consumers, and the wider community. One of the most vital relationships in the sustainable-agri business is with local markets and restaurants. Let's delve deeply into the process of building these connections, offering insights and advice on creating fruitful partnerships and fostering a circular local economy.

9.1. Identifying Potential Partners

The first step in building relationships is identification of potential partners who are likely to appreciate and resonate with your farming values. Start by creating a list of local markets, restaurants, and cafes that have a focus on local, organic, or sustainable food. Do a bit of research into their sourcing policies and learn about their customer base. You should aim to work with those establishments that value quality, sustainability, and community engagement, as these are the pillars of the farm-to-table model.

Understanding their goals and challenges will allow you to determine how best you can offer value to them. Keep in mind that this process is not just about selling your produce; it's about creating long-standing relationships that help foster a culture of sustainability within your community.

9.2. Approaching Your Prospective Partners

Once you've identified potential partners, it's time to make your approach. Remember, you're not just selling a product, you're selling a story – the story of your farm, your practices, and your commitment to sustainability.

In your initial approach, communicate your offer clearly and convincingly. Provide details about the types of crops you grow, your growing techniques, the quality of the produce and importantly, your sustainable farming practices. Using visual aids like photographs of your farm and produce, or even inviting potential partners for a tour could immensely help in driving home your point.

9.3. Building Trust and Collaboration

Trust is the cornerstone of any business relationship. It's important to ensure reliability in terms of quality and quantity of your produce. Always strive to maintain transparency with regards to your farming practices and conditions. Provide regular updates and invite them to visit your farm. Collaboration too plays an important role. Engage in open dialogue regarding their needs and adjustments you can make to your produce or practices to better meet their requirements.

9.4. Structuring Agreements

While verbal agreements can work for smaller, less formal partnerships, it's best to have a written agreement or contract once you begin dealing with more substantial amounts. The terms of agreement should detail conditions for supply, quality, quantity, pricing, delivery, and payment arrangements. These agreements protect the interests of both parties and provide a framework for resolving any disputes that may arise.

9.5. Sustaining Relationships

Building the relationship is just the first part; sustaining it is an ongoing process. Regular follow-ups, open communication channels, receptiveness to feedback, and continuous reassurance of your commitment to the highest quality and sustainable practices will cement your relationship with your partners. Regularly updating them about what's happening on your farm creates a sense of partnership and community connection.

9.6. Expanding Your Network

As you build and sustain relationships with your local markets and restaurants, new opportunities can emerge to expand your network. Trade fairs, farmers' markets, local festivals and events are excellent platforms to connect with potential collaborators. Additionally, workshops and seminars on sustainable agriculture can help you meet like-minded individuals and potential business partners.

Sustainable farming isn't just about the farm; it's about the relationships you cultivate along the way. By connecting with local markets and restaurants, you're not only growing your business but also sowing seeds within the community, embedding your produce in the local food culture, and being a major component of the drive towards a sustainable future. Remember - a successful farming business is as much about the strength of your crops as it is about the strength of your relationships. Build them mindfully and nurture them with care, and you'll reap a rich, interconnected harvest.

Chapter 10. Marketing Your Farm-to-Table Business

In this chapter, we will break down the importance of marketing your farm-to-table business, teasing out the optimal strategies to maximize visibility, engagement, and ultimately, customer loyalty and sales. In a world where sustainability and local sourcing are treasured, it's crucial to leverage these elements effectively in your marketing strategies. By understanding the best channels and resources, you can position your farm-to-table business in a way that not just attracts customers, but retains them too.

===Understanding Your Target Market

The first and perhaps most critical step in marketing is identifying your target audience. Whether it's health-conscious consumers, local restaurants, or farmer's market enthusiasts, it's vital to understand who you're communicating with and what their needs and preferences are. Once you identify these individuals, you can tailor your content and messaging to suit their tastes. Ensure to establish:

- Demographics (age, income, gender, location)

- Buying behavior (purchase triggers, habits)

- Needs and preferences (taste, freshness, organic, local)

- Communication channels (social media, email newsletters, local papers)

Gathering this information allows you to develop an in-depth consumer profile that will guide all your ensuing marketing efforts.

===Crafting Your Unique Selling Proposition

A unique selling proposition (USP) differentiates you from competitors. It's the unique benefit or set of benefits your customers receive when they buy from you. In a farm-to-table business, this could include factors like:

- Locally sourced produce
- Organic certification
- Produce variety
- Sustainability initiatives
- Community involvement

Establish your USP and ensure it's communicated effectively throughout your marketing platforms.

===Building a Brand

Your brand is your business's personality. It should reflect your values and resonate with your target audience. In farm-to-table businesses, customers often associate brands with values like sustainability, community, health, and localism. Reflect these values in your logo, color palette, typography, and language you use to communicate with your audience. Building a recognizable and trusted brand paves the way for long-term customer loyalty.

===Choosing Your Marketing Channels

Marketing channels are the mediums you use to communicate with your audience. Here's a breakdown of some channels that might be effective:

1. Social Media: Platforms such as Facebook, Instagram, and Twitter are wonderful tools for sharing your story, connecting with your customers, and showcasing your products. Consider a mix of organic posts and paid advertising for maximum reach.

2. Email Marketing: Regular newsletters can keep your audience engaged and informed about your products, special offers, and events.

3. Local Press: Feature in community newspapers, magazines, or radio shows to reach a broader local audience.

4. Community Events: Participating in or hosting farm-to-table dinners, farmers markets, or educational workshops can help raise awareness and build a reputable image.

===Implementing a Marketing Plan

Once you've established your target demographic, USP, brand, and marketing channels, it's time to implement your plan. Also, ensure to measure your marketing performance regularly to identify areas of improvement and enhance your strategies for better results.

===Local Partnerships and Collaborations

Forming partnerships with other local businesses, particularly those who share your target market, can be an excellent way to expand your reach. Similarly, participation in community events and supporting local causes can positively affect your reputation and visibility.

In this chapter, we've gone through the fundamentals of marketing a farm-to-table business—defining your target market, crafting a unique selling proposition, building a memorable brand, choosing the most productive marketing channels, implementing your plan, and exploiting local partnerships and collaborations. Each of these elements has its own depth, so explore them, experiment, and find what resonates most with your business model and customers. Happy farming and marketing!

Remember, marketing isn't a one-off effort; it's a continuous process that needs nurturing. Just like your crops, it requires care, patience, and an understanding of the environment. As your business grows and evolves, so should your marketing strategies. Keep your eyes on your business's vision, stay grounded in your values, and you're sure to harvest the fruits of your labor.

Chapter 11. Planning for the Future: Scaling and Sustainability

In the journey of creating a sustainable agri-business, there comes a point when mere sustenance transitions into ambitious growth. This chapter is dedicated to that exciting pivot - a comprehensive look at scaling your operation and ensuring its long-lasting sustainability.

11.1. Know Your Aims and Set Your Goals

First and foremost, your plan for scaling and sustainability needs clear, concrete goals. Are you looking to increase your yield, branch out into new markets, or launch new, value-added products? Your objectives must be clear and followed by an elaborate strategy to bring them to fruition. It's the same approach one would use in any business sector, but in the context of sustainable farming, your goals should also address both your environmental and social impact.

11.2. Increasing Your Yield

When looking to upscale your yield, it can be tempting to default to traditional methods like using more land or more labor. Sustainable farming, however, means thinking differently. Consider the implementation of practices like intercropping, crop rotation, or agroforestry. These have been proven to not only increase yield, but also improve soil health and resilience.

Automatic systems for irrigation or the deployment of greenhouses can also be beneficial. In making such decisions, ensure you maintain the balance between increasing productivity and preserving environmental integrity.

11.3. Expanding Your Market

Which outlets are ripe for your goods? Don't just think about grocery stores. Restaurants, schools, hospitals, and other institutions often source from local farms. Online sales platforms – both general and food-specific – can open up new, direct-to-consumer avenues. Another viable avenue is community-supported agriculture (CSA) schemes, allowing local customers to "subscribe" to a season's worth of produce.

When planning your market expansion, be sure to remember the core tenets of sustainable farming. This encourages not just organic production methods, but local consumption too, reducing food miles and fostering local economies.

11.4. Introducing Value-added Products

Adding value to your raw farm products can be a huge boon to your business. This doesn't mean compromising on your eco-ethos, however. From organic jams and juices made from your fruits to compost sold from your farm's waste, the possibilities are many and varied.

11.5. Calculating the Costs

It's also essential to understand that scaling often involves increased expenses – at least initially. More crops can mean more inputs and labor. Expanding to new markets may involve more transportation or packaging. And value-added products require their own set of resources, potentially including new equipment, regulatory approval, or branding efforts.

11.6. Maintaining Sustainability

While scaling, maintaining sustainability is also of prime importance. Here, transparency in your operations will be key. Not only will it reassure your customers, but it'll also enable a constant re-evaluation of your practices to ensure they're truly sustainable.

To do this, you need to have in depth knowledge of your supply chain. You need to know where your seeds come from, how your processes may affect the local water sources, or the working conditions of your labor force.

11.7. Using Technology

Technology is a potent tool you can employ to assist in maintaining complete transparency. With the help of technology in farming – known as AgTech – you can streamline your farm operations, improve efficiencies, and even educate yourself and others about better farming practices.

11.8. Securing Sustainable Certification

Obtaining certification such as USDA Organic or being part of the Fair Trade movement can be a significant stamp of approval for your operation. It can validate your sustainable practices and aide in marketing your products.

11.9. Final Thoughts

Scaling and sustainability are not mutually exclusive. With a clear vision of your goals, an understanding of your costs, and a commitment to transparency, you can grow your farm-to-table business without compromising on its environmental or social responsibility. Remember, sustainable farming is about feeding the world, strengthening local communities, and securing the future of our planet. With careful planning and thoughtful execution, your business can contribute towards all these aims.

www.ingramcontent.com/pod-product-compliance
Lightning Source LLC
Chambersburg PA
CBHW072221290526
45794CB00007B/2843